ROLANDO FUSI

LOOKING AT
FLORENCE

BONECHI EDITORE - FIRENZE

PREFACE

Translation from the Italian by MICHAEL HOLLINGWORTH

The technical progress of the last twenty years, the increased rapidity and efficiency of means of transport and greater general prosperity have led more and more people to satisfy the " complex of Ulysses " — to travel, to see, to know.

The romantic image of the highly informed traveller, an expert in art and history, is gradually disappearing, to be replaced by that of the modern man, with a wider range of interests, whose culture or specialised field of knowledge often has nothing to do with Dante or Michelangelo.

The visitor to Italy today thus has a new set of requirements: travelling no longer seems to mean the confirmation at first-hand of knowledge already acquired, but rather a direct process of discovery which may subsequently lead to further inquiry and studies (at least, it is to be hoped so).

In the necessary choice from among the thousands of pictures of Florence which were available, I have kept these considerations above all in mind, while naturally laying stress on the greatest masterpieces and illustrating their various aspects according to a priority expressed by the visitors to Florence themselves, in the past fifteen years passed in their company.

The text, containing basic information, is easy to read, and should allow each visitor to make a pleasant personal acquaintance, on the spot, with the works of art. At the same time, the exceptionally good quality of the illustrations means that when he returns home he will be able to renew this acquaintance and the memory of his visit.

Special thanks go to the publishers Bonechi, always competent and sensitive to the need for a continuous, and in this case considerable, effort to keep up with the requirements of the many welcome visitors to the city of Florence.

The Author

FLORENCE:
A HISTORICAL
OUTLINE

When the legionaries of Octavian, some 40 years B.C., gave the name of " Florentia " to their colony north of Rome, they could never have imagined that many centuries later it would become such a famous and important city. And indeed more than 1300 years were to pass before Florence entered its period of greatest magnificence. It was strategically situated, and had convenient river access to the sea, widespread trading interests and an extremely strong currency (the 24-carat gold " florin ", named after the city): these factors contributed to a political, intellectual and artistc leadership so considerable that the world has to this day remained indebted to Florence in every field of learning.

It had already become a Roman municipality in the 1st century A.D., and it later became the most important centre in the region of Tuscany. It survived throughout the darkest eras of the Middle Ages to revive slowly in the age of the Carolingian emperors. Then followed the rule of the Marchesa Matilda of Tuscany and the struggles against both the powerful clergy and the feudal lords, until by 1115 the political entity of the free " Commune " of Florence was virtually an established fact. Ten years later the originally Etruscan city of Fiesole, from which Florence's first settlers had come, fell under its domination.

But within the city, surrounded by its new walls, the first conflicts between rich aristocrats and artisans soon broke out: this was the period of the Guilds or professional corporations, and of the bitter struggles between the Guelphs, supporters of the Pope, and the Ghibellines, followers of the Emperor. In 1303 the poet Dante Alighieri, a " White Guelph ", was forced to leave Florence to go into exile at Ravenna. In the meantime, Florence's power was steadily growing. Its territory was enlarged, and it conquered Pistoia, Arezzo and Siena, so that by the end of the 14th century it was one of the most important cities in Italy.

This was the era of Dante, Boccaccio and Giotto. It was also the era of Florence's burgeoning wool and silk industries and of its powerful companies of bankers and merchants. Among the latter, the family of the Medici gradually gained greater and greater economic power and political influence. The " Signoria ", or political domination, of the Medici was established by Cosimo the Elder, who was later succeeded by that acute politician and patron of the arts, Lorenzo the Magnificent. The era of Lorenzo in the 15th century was indeed one of the most magnificent in the entire history of Florence, especially for its art, culture and science.

His era saw the birth of Humanism, or the Renaissance, in which the cultural energies of Italy were freed from the domination of the monasteries and

the courts. The Renaissance also affirmed the positive aspect of man's role on earth as king of his universe and an emanation of the divine, and led to the abandonment of the old, dogmatic way of learning in favour of the empirical, scientific method. The beginning of this period was dominated by figures like Alberti, Brunelleschi, Botticelli and Savonarola, followed by others such as Michelangelo, Leonardo, Machiavelli and Galileo, indeed by so many men of genius that it seems hardly possible that one city should have given birth to so many.

Today the city of Florence stands on the banks of the Arno where once, in distant times, there was only a swamp. Elegant and rather proud of its splendid past, it is surrounded by green hills, a ramification of the Apennine Mountains. Most noticeable on the hills are the tall, dark form of the cypress and the silver-grey of the olive trees, typical of the Tuscan countryside. As to the city, one's first impression is of its pleasant yellow tones: the earth from Siena gives almost all its buildings this warm, gilded hue. The gilded effect stands out among the Renaissance buildings, the apses of the churches and the bridges over the Arno, against the grey of the sandstone. The

facades of the churches create a different effect again with their shining marble: the white stone from Carrara, green from Prato and red from Siena. Most imposing of all are the Cathedral, Santa Maria del Fiore, and Giotto's Bell-tower next to it, soaring above the lesser symbols of Florence's magnificence. Not far from these is the Palazzo Vecchio, with its severe, fortified aspect, the administrative heart of the city for many centuries and today the seat of the Mayor. Further on again is the Church of Santa Croce which contains the remains of such great men as Michelangelo, Galileo, Machiavelli and Rossini.

Other Romanesque and Gothic towers can be seen above the red tiled roofs of the historical centre, with its houses built one against the other, divided by dark and narrow alleyways, sometimes built around gardens but more often containing simple courtyards. They are houses built on human dimensions, three or four storeys high, so that there is none of the effect of alienation typical of the huge metropolis. Florence's beauty is undeniable, the result of a perfect harmony between nature and art, of the classical Renaissance balance which this city taught to the world.

THE CATHEDRAL: SANTA MARIA DEL FIORE

The Cathedral, the religious centre of Florence, is so huge that only a bird's eye view can give a real idea of it in its entirety. The building space within the walls of Florence had already become restricted in 1350, even before the walls themselves were finished. All medieval cities, but Florence in particular, suffered from this "hunger for space". Furthermore, as to the Cathedral, the Florentine Republic had decided that it must be "of the greatest magnificence that can be conceived of, as great and as beautiful as the efforts and strength of man can create". This partly explains why the church is almost suffocated by the smaller buildings which crowd round it, unlike other such churches in Rome, Milan or Pisa for example.

The architect Arnolfo di Cambio began work on the Cathedral in 1296, laying its foundations on the remains of a previous Cathedral, Santa Reparata,

parts of which have been brought to light by recent excavations. On the death of Arnolfo in 1302 work was interrupted, to be resumed in 1334 under the direction of Giotto who already had charge of the building of the Bell-tower. When Giotto too died in 1337, the project again lost momentum, but between 1357 and 1364 Lapo Ghini and Francesco Talenti were given charge of the building, which was to be even more grandiose than in Arnolfo's original conception. In fact the final plans for the Cathedral were presented by four architects in 1366, and building went ahead more rapidly. By 1378 the vault above the central nave was already completed, and between 1380 and 1421 the apse and the tambour below the cupola were constructed. In 1436 Pope Eugene IV consecrated the Cathedral, dedicating it to Santa Maria del Fiore (" St. Mary of the Flower "). Work on the cupola was completed by the placing of the gilded copper ball, cast by Andrea del Verrocchio, on the top of the lantern. This occurred on 30 May 1471, so that 173 years had passed from the beginning of construction.

Among the various important historical events which took place in the Cathedral was the Conspiracy of the Pazzi (at Eastertime, 26 April 1478), in which Giuliano dei Medici was killed and his brother Lor-

enzo the Magnificent wounded. And here, between 1497 and 1498 Girolamo Savonarola, who was later executed, delivered his fiery sermons.

The Cathedral's facade was erected by the architect Emilio de Fabris, who designed it with the original decorations in Florentine Gothic style in mind and supervised work on it from 1871 to 1883, in the era during which Florence was capital of Italy.

On the pediment can be seen the busts of distinguished Florentine citizens. Under the splendid rose-window, in the niches, are the Madonna Enthroned between the Apostles. The central portal in bronze, as well as the relief of Our Lady in Glory in the cusp above it, are by Augusto Passaglia (1895-1903). In the niche beside the main door is a statue of Pope Eugene VI, who consecrated the Cathedral to Our Lady in 1412.

LO SCOPPIO DEL CARRO

" EXPLOSION OF THE CART "

The picture shows the end of this celebration, which takes place each year on Holy Saturday and in which fireworks are exploded to celebrate the Resurrection of Christ. The ceremony, the origin of which goes far back in time, is extremely picturesque and includes a procession of people carrying ancient weapons and dressed in period costume.

INTERIOR OF THE CATHEDRAL

One immediately notices the great contrast between the exterior of the Cathedral, with its exuberant, almost Eastern decoration, and the sober and severe interior. This contrast is due to various factors. One is the great difference between the building materials: marbles of various colours are used on the outside walls and the floor, but the basic structure of the Cathedral is in hard sandstone. The interior of this magnificent example of Florentine Gothic architecture is vast but soberly decorated, in keeping with the character of the Florentines themselves who wanted a Cathedral without frivolous ornamentation, but one that was grandiose and austere so that the people could gather there in large numbers. Along the left-hand wall can be seen the huge detached frescoes by Andrea del Castagno and Paolo Uccello, depicting respectively Niccolò da Tolentino (1456) and John Hawkwood (1436), military leaders who served the Florentine Republic. Further on is a table painted by Domenico de Michelino (1465), which shows Dante Alighieri with his poem, the "Divine Comedy" and the city of Florence in the background at right. These works of art testify not only to the faith of the Florentines but to their pride in being citizens of Florence. Indeed, the name of the Cathedral itself, Santa Maria del Fiore ("St. Mary of the Flower"), alludes to the lily, the symbol of the city, which is depicted on the tops of the arches on the left of the central nave and in the cupola. The marble choir was made by Baccio Bandinelli and Giovanni dell'Opera on a commission from Cosimo I dei Medici; it replaced the former choir which was made from wood and was much smaller. The Cathedral is designed in the form of a cross, and the wings of the cross contain three apses, with five chapels in each one. Above the bronze doors of the two sacristies can be seen the Resurrection and the Ascension of Christ, two magnificent glazed terra-cotta works by Luca della Robbia (1447).

The remains of the original Cathedral of Florence, Santa Reparata, brought to light recently by excavations. They can be seen beneath the floor level of the present Cathedral of Santa Maria del Fiore.

Pietà by Michelangelo

Of the four **Pietà** by Michelangelo, the one in the Cathedral of Florence is the third: he sculpted it between the ages of 75 and 80 for his own tomb. (The first **Pietà** is that in St. Peter's at Rome, recently damaged by a fanatic, the second is in the Academy Gallery in Florence, and the fourth is in the Sforza Castle in Milan). This third **Pietà** is perhaps the most dramatic of all. The lifeless body of Christ in the centre of the work sags heavily, with the head falling towards his Mother; the features of the head are barely sketched in the stone as if the artistic process had been frozen by the pain. Above, as Nicodemus, is the self-portrait of the artist, who thus participates in the divine tragedy. Mary Magdalene on the left was completed by Calcagni and seems colder and more conventional, as if a spectator rather than participant in the drama. Over the centuries the marble has acquired a golden patina which makes it almost resemble ivory.

THE CUPOLA

In 1418, when construction of the Cathedral's apse had been almost completed, a competition was announced for the erection of the cupola; it was won, among criticisms and some confusion, by Filippo Brunelleschi. He erected this revolutionary structure between 1420 and 1436, first adding to the beauty of the church's proportions by constructing a tambour 49 feet high at the base of the ovoid-shaped cupola, which was designed in such a way as to avoid the need for reinforcement or scaffolding. The cupola has double walls: between the inside wall and the roof outside are the stairs by which one ascends to the lantern at the top. The original wooden model of Brunelleschi's project is still kept in the Cathedral's museum. Michelangelo himself took his inspiration from this masterpiece to design the cupola of St. Peter's in Rome.

Brunelleschi's cupola is 370 feet high including the lantern and has a diameter of 146 feet. From the top of it there is a magnificent view of the city of Florence.

THE BAPTISTRY

The origins of the Baptistry dedicated to San Giovanni Battista (St. John the Baptist), standing in front of the Cathedral, are lost in time. Once thought to date from the 5th century, it is now generally held to be a Romanesque construction of the 11th or 12th century. Originally the external walls of the building were in sandstone, but later they were dressed with the white marble of Carrara and the green marble of Prato, and the double order of pillars which support decorative arches similar to those of the Church of San Miniato al Monte was added. The Baptistry stands on the remains of a Paleochristian church, and in its foundations have been found traces of a Roman building and mosaics, recently brought to light again. San Giovanni was first the Cathedral of Florence, and became its Baptistry only in 1128 after the city's population had doubled and thus needed a larger church. At one time the children of the Florentines were baptised in San Giovanni on two occasions during the year, and a black bean was deposited for every male child and a white bean for each female child, thus permitting a census to be made of the city's population. St. John the Baptist remains the patron saint of Florence, and there is a festival with fireworks and a procession from the Cathedral to the Baptistry held in his honour on 24 June every year. The Baptistry is without doubt the finest example of Tuscan Romanesque architecture on an octagonal plan. Its three doors, which correspond to three points of the compass, are also of great artistic importance.

INTERIOR OF THE BAPTISTRY

It is built on an octagonal plan and has two architectural orders. These consist of the lower part, which has granite columns with gilded capitals alternating with pillars, and the upper part between whose smaller pillars are the windows of the so-called women's gallery where the women once sat during religious services, separated from the men. The combination of the decorative motifs on the floor and on the walls creates a striking impression of sober harmony. Entering by the door made by Andrea Pisano, one can see on the left the wooden statue of Mary Magdalene by Donatello, conceived with exceptional realism, then the funeral monument to the anti-pope John XXIII, Baldassarre Coscia, of Naples, who was elected at Bologna by sixteen cardinals but later renounced his claims at the feet of Pope Martin V. The monument, a fine work bt Donatello and Michelozzo (1435), stands harmoniously in the space between the two columns. The baptismal fount once stood in the centre of the building in the area which is now without marble decoration; the present-day fount, which is smaller and stands to the right as one enters, dates from the 14th century and was made out of a single block of marble.

MOSAICS OF THE CUPOLA

On the triumphal arch of the apse and on the cupola are splendid mosaics in rather Byzantine style, done by various Venetian and Florentine artists in the 13th and 14th centuries. The mosaics in the apse were begun in 1225 by Iacopo da Torrita. Those on the cupola date

from the 14th century, and among those who collaborated on the work were Cimabue, Andrea Tafi and Gaddi. The subjects are taken from the book of Genesis and the lives of Joseph, Christ and John the Baptist. The apse is dominated by the huge figure of Christ the Saviour (23 feet in diameter), surrounded by angels in judgment, while below right are the sinners condemned to Hell.

The splendid mosaic decorations of the cupola remind us that this sort of " wall painting ", using small cubes of a glass compound substance, is of ancient origin. The art reached its period of maximum splendour from the 4th to the 7th centuries, when it was used to adorn the naves but above all the apses of the early Byzantine churches. By the skilful use of the various colours of the tesserae, as the pieces of glass are called, the maximum artistic or decorative effect possible was obtained. At the same time, the curves and irregularities in the surface of the walls were exploited through their different reflection of the light to create vibrant and luminous effects. In contrast, modern mosaics are less effective, in that they often use a huge variety of colours with the sole aim of perfectly imitating the art of oil painting, a far cry from the mosaic's original role.

The dome of the Baptistry was once open like that of the Pantheon in Rome, but it was closed in 1550. Its decoration can be summarily divided into five sections. From bottom to top, apart from the " Last Judgment ", these are:

1) **Life of St. John the Baptist.**
2) **Life of the Redeemer.**
3) **Life of Joseph.**
4) **The Creation of the World.**
5) **Executors of the Divine Will.**

At the top of the cupola is a splendid frieze.

THE "GATE OF PARADISE"

This is the eastern door of the Baptistry, which Michelangelo defined as fit to be the "gate of Paradise". It represents the masterpiece of Lorenzo Ghiberti, who worked on it for 27 years, from 1425 to 1452, lavishing on it all the richness of his imagination, combined with a fine sense of composition and profound knowledge of the modeller's art. Michelozzo, Benozzo Gozzoli and Bernardo Cennini collaborated with him on the work. The door, a universally admired masterpiece, has ten panels depicting Biblical scenes, the themes of which were decided by Leonardo Bruni. In the part illustrated are stories from the lives of Jacob and Esau, showing clearly the brilliant modelling technique and perfect perspective, so that the figures stand out against the architectural background and the work seems almost a painting in bronze. At the centre of the door at left is the self-portrait of Ghiberti. The door's original gilding has recently been recovered from beneath the patina formed over the centuries. It was badly damaged by Florence's flood in 1966 when the waters of the Arno reached a height of more than 6 feet.

THE SOUTHERN DOOR was designed by Andrea Pisano in 1339 and has 28 bas-reliefs depicting stories of St. John the Baptist and the theological virtues. The door is a fine late Gothic work. The three statues above, showing the beheading of St. John the Baptist, are by Vincenzo Danti (1571).

THE NORTHERN DOOR is also by Ghiberti, who spent 25 years on it — from 1401 (date of the famous competition) until 1425. It too is divided into 28 panels, depicting stories from the life of Christ and the Doctors of the Church. Above the door, " St. John Preaching " (1510), by F. Rustici, a pupil of Leonardo.

GIOTTO'S BELL-TOWER

The 265ft. high bell-tower is still today, more than 500 years after it was built, perhaps the finest work of its kind in the world. Giotto submitted its design on the invitation of Florence's governing body in 1334, and work was begun on the huge structure's foundations in July of the same year. Unfortunately three years later Giotto died, and the work was continued by Andrea Pisano until 1348, being completed by Francesco Talenti in 1359. Both adhered scrupulously to the design of the tower done by their great predecessor, with the sole exception of the final spire which would have added more than 90 feet to the height of the tower but which was never erected. From the tower's terrace, reached by climbing up 414 steps, there is a splendid panoramic view of Florence.

PALAZZO MEDICI RICCARDI

When the first Medici ruler, Cosimo the Elder, returned to Florence from exile, he decided to have a palatial residence constructed which would be worthy of his family's position though not excessively luxurious so as not to arouse the people's jealousy. He therefore commissioned the architect Michelozzo Michelozzi who began work on the building in 1440 and brought it to completion twenty years later. The residence remains today, along with Palazzo Pitti and Palazzo Strozzi, one of the finest and most typical examples of aristocratic Florentine architecture from the early Renaissance. The severe effect of the projecting ashlar stonework decreases gracefully towards the top of the building. The large windows at ground level are protected by gratings while on the upper floors are elegant mullioned windows. The roof is finished with a fine cornice. The two large windows at the corner of the building were at one time entranceways to a private loggia.

Lorenzo the Magnificent and Catherine dei Medici were both born in this building, and the young Michelangelo lived here for a time when he was a pupil of Bertoldo. The fine courtyard is decorated with graffiti and marble sculptures depicting mythological subjects; under its gallery are numerous tombstones and inscriptions from the Roman era. In the building's private chapel is the famous "Cavalcade of the Magi", the masterpiece of Benozzo Gozzoli (1460). Among the historical figures who can be recognised in this work are the Byzantine emperor from Constantinople, John VII Paleologus, Lorenzo the Magnificent and Sigismondo Malatesta, as well as the painter himself.

PIAZZA SAN LORENZO
Central market

This architectural complex includes the Church of San Lorenzo, the Laurentian Library, the cloisters, the Old and New Sacristies and the Chapel of the Princes. In front of the church, where the stalls of the market begin, one can see the statue of Giovanni delle Bande Nere, the Medici family's famous military leader, a work by Baccio Bandinelli (1540). The statue was placed in this position in 1870 during the period when Florence was capital of Italy and the central market was built. In recent years the market has become much larger; as well as the food market, it has numerous stalls which sell the work of Florence's craftsmen.

CHURCH OF
SAN LORENZO

The original Church of San Lorenzo was consecrated in 393 by San Lorenzo da Ambrogio, bishop of Milan, which is why it is also called the " Basilica Ambrosiana ". The present church dates back to 1423 when Brunelleschi was commissioned by Giovanni di Bicci dei Medici to direct its construction. After the church and the Old Sacristy by Brunelleschi, the library and the New Sacristy, designed by Michelangelo, and later the Chapel of the Princes, were constructed.

The interior in grey sandstone is one of the first fine products of the genius of Filippo Brunelleschi, whose tomb was recently found during excavations below the floor of the Cathedral. The classical, monumental style of the ancient Roman forums and triumphal arches is translated here into a style with more human dimensions. The elegant round sandstone arches are supported by columns with Corinthian capitals. The lacunar ceiling above the central nave, with the coat-of-arms of the Medici in the centre, is illuminated by the church's tall windows.

THE
MEDICI CHAPELS

One enters the Chapel of the Princes and Michelangelo's New Sacristy from Piazza della Madonna degli Aldobrandini, behind the church. Passing through the crypt where most of the Medici grand dukes and members of their families are buried, one reaches the upper floor of the Chapel of the Princes. Construction of this grandiose chapel was begun in 1604 by Matteo Nigetti to a design by the Medici noble, Don Giovanni, who planned it as a burial place for his family worthy of their power and greatness. It should be noted that the chapel was never entirely completed: the altar is partly made of wood painted to imitate marble and some of the statues depicting the Medici grand

dukes are lacking. The chapel is decorated with hundreds of different marbles and precious and semi-precious stones which were brought from all over the world. The sarcophagi are made from Egyptian granite and green jasper from Corsica (note that the bodies are in the crypt). The Medici escutcheons above are in red and yellow jasper from Cyprus. Around the base of the Chapel, made from granite from Elba and jasper from Sicily, are the sixteen coats-of-arms of the cities in the Grand-Duchy of Tuscany, made from semi-precious stones, coral, lapus lazuli and mother-of-pearl. Above each coat-of-arms is the name of the city to which it belongs. The working of precious and semi-precious stones and the art of using them for inlays or mosaics were developed to create the decorations of this chapel and these later became typical products of Florence's artists and craftsmen. The gilt bronze statues in the niches of the chapel are by Tacca (1640). The frescoes in the cupola are by Pietro Benvenuti (1828) and depict such episodes as the Creation, the Original Sin and the Death of Abel. The overall impression which the chapel creates is one of pomp and funereal splendour.

FLORENTIAE·CIVITAS

THE NEW SACRISTY

This sacristy, which is actually another funerary chapel, was built by Michelangelo Buonarroti for Pope Clement VII. It is the only work by Michelangelo where seven statues can be seen placed in their architectural environment by the artist himself. Work on the sacristy was begun in 1520 and completed sixteen years later. The great Michelangelo sought to give it, both in its architecture and in its sculpture, a grandiose, solemn atmosphere. The square room, with its imposing cupola, is full of the sensation of movement and every architectural element emphasises the plastic energy of its forms. The profound meaning which the chapel is intended to convey is one of meditation on the eternity of time

compared with the brevity of human life. It was believed at the time that the sun rotated around the earth: Michelangelo sculpted four allegorical figures, representing Day, Night, Dawn and Dusk, and placed them on two sarcophagi to indicate the eternal passing of time — time, the judge and ruler of man's actions and thoughts, whether he be general or philosopher. At the same time, the great weight of the two figures seals the tomb shut. The sculptural group depicting Our Lady with Saints Cosma and Damian stands above the mortal remains of Lorenzo the Magnificent and his brother Giuliano. The New Sacristy presents us with a Michelangelo at once architect and sculptor. But the two roles merge into one, since the individual works gain from their environment as well as contributing to it: architecture and sculpture in the chapel are complementary, making up an artistic whole.

Tomb of Giuliano, Duke of Nemours

(1479-1516)

The sarcophagus is made from Carrara marble, and it is interesting to note that in the ellipse-shaped cover whose volutes fold over the lower part one can see the same line to be found again in the arches of the Bridge of Santa Trinita, built later by Ammannati. Here lie the remains of Giuliano, Duke of Nemours, son of Lorenzo the Magnificent and brother of Pope Leo X, depicted in the niche above as a Roman general, dressed in armour and holding the commander's baton, symbol of the man of action. At his feet are the symbolic figures of Day and Night. The uncompleted head of Day, looking over his massively muscular shoulder, seems to radiate energy. Symbols of obscurity can be seen below the figure of the woman representing Night, with its highly polished marble.

Tomb of Lorenzo, Duke of Urbino

(1492-1519)

Lorenzo, son of Pietro, nephew of Pope Leo X and father of Catherine dei Medici, is depicted in a meditative attitude. It was to Lorenzo that Florence's political genius Niccolò Macchiavelli dedicated " The Prince ", a political tract based in part on the principle that the " end justifies the means ". The two figures on this tomb symbolise Dusk and Dawn; a splendid detail of the latter can be seen at right.

Tomb of Lorenzo the Magnificent and Giuliano de' Medici

The **STATUES OF SAINTS COSMA AND DAMIAN** were done by Montorsoli and Raffaello da Montelupo, following models by Michelangelo. In the **Madonna and Child,** one of the most famous works by Michelangelo himself, the Virgin seems already aware of the tragic destiny of her Son, and the Christ Child seems somehow more human than the traditional crowned figure in the act of blessing.

THE CUPOLA, with its odd, trapezoid-shaped windows and lacunar ceiling in which the lacunars are smaller towards the top, gives the optical impression of soaring upwards, which is yet another product of the architectural genius of Michelangelo.

PIAZZA SANTISSIMA ANNUNZIATA

This is the Florentine square which expresses most of all the Renaissance spirit, with that perfect equilibrium of dimensions and serene sense of measure which have come to seem typical of Florentine Renaissance architecture. To the right of the church's portico can be seen the Hospital of the Innocents, one of the first buildings produced by the Renaissance, a masterpiece designed by Brunelleschi and erected by him between 1421 and 1424. The hospital was constructed as a refuge for orphans and abandoned children. It stands above a low flight of steps, and the spaces between its nine harmonious arches are decorated with terra-cotta tondoes by Andrea della Robbia, which depict babies symbolically seeking the charity of Florence's rich.

GALLERY OF THE ACADEMY OF FINE ARTS

The Academy of Fine Arts, founded by Cosimo I dei Medici in 1562, was considerably expanded 200 years later under the Grand-Duke Pietro Leopoldo. In 1784 in fact the building was enlarged to its present dimensions so as to bring together under its roof all the drawing schools in Florence, as well as the conservatory and the Academy Gallery. The aim of the gallery was to provide a collection of works of art which could be directly studied by the student artists. The gallery acquired even greater importance in 1873 when the original of Michelangelo's **David** was transferred here from Piazza della Signoria to protect it from the weather. Today, apart from the **David,** the gallery houses the **Pietà di Palestrina,** the four **Prisoners** and the **St. Matthew** by Michelangelo. It also has an important collection of paintings and Flemish tapestries.

THE "DAVID"

When, on 16 August 1501, Michelangelo accepted the commission to sculpt the **David,** he was not yet famous and successful. He had done several bas-reliefs, the **Bacchus,** the wooden crucifix and his first **Pietà.** But apparently no one in Rome could believe that the **Pietà** (still in St. Peter's) was done by a Florentine only 24 years old, and this presumably led Michelangelo to sign the work — the only one which carries his name. When he returned to Florence he put forward his idea for the **David,** the Biblical hero who killed Goliath to liberate his country, just as the Florentines were ready to defend the institutions and the liberty of their city. The political symbol proved stimulating, Michelangelo received the commission to sculpt the statue, and completed it after about three years' work.

In April 1504 the statue was ceremoniously placed in Piazza della Signoria in front of the Palazzo Vecchio, by unanimous decision of a committee consisting of eminent citizens and artists, among them Botticelli and Leonardo da Vinci. Michelangelo was 30 years old. In 1527, during a siege of the Palazzo Vecchio, a heavy object falling from above broke off the statue's right arm, which was later restored. In 1873, in order to protect it from further damage by the elements (as can be seen, the toes of the left foot were already considerably eaten away), the architect De Fabris designed the special stand in the Academy for the **David,** studying questions of light and space so as to permit its maximum appreciation.

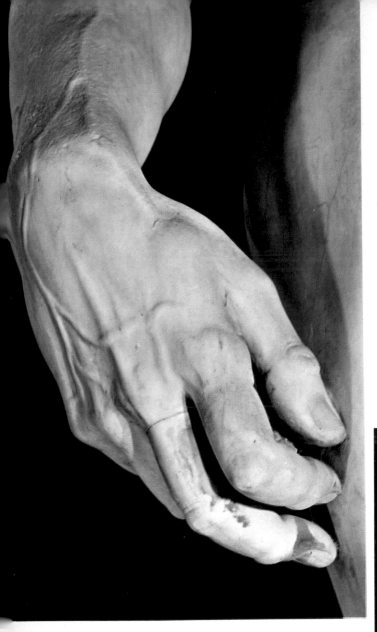

weight on the right leg, despite the splendid prominence given to the anatomical features and the dynamic tension visible in every part. In the right hand and arm, in the ribs and the abdomen, Michelangelo achieved a level of realism never seen before. In the face (one must move to the right-hand side of the stand to see it) there is a combination of pride and moral strength. The forehead and mouth express unyielding determination, and the eyes seem to burn with an inner fire. The **David** was created in the era of Amerigo Vespucci, Columbus, Machiavelli and Leonardo da Vinci. The statue thus represents more than just David, more than Apollo or even Hercules: in the end it is Michelangelo's monument glorifying the Renaissance man.

It seems strange now to record that when the statue was first placed in Piazza della Signoria it received more blame than praise. Somebody said that it was too big (it stands more than 13 feet high) because the Bible described David as less than 13 years old. Another remarked that the right hand was too large: the veins of this hand are noticeably filled with blood compared with the other hand, perhaps partly to counterbalance the weight of the left arm. And finally the Gonfaloniere of Florence, Piero Soderini, had his say pronouncing that the nose was too big!

From a frontal position, the **David** seems almost relaxed, with the

The "Pietà" di Palestrina

This **Pietà,** which was originally in the chapel of the Palazzo Barberini at Palestrina, near Rome, was recently moved to the Academy Gallery. The attribution of the dramatic group to Michelangelo is still being discussed, since the work is not even mentioned in the various and detailed biographies of the artist. But if not by Michelangelo's own hand, it was certainly inspired by the work he did in the final period of his life. Worth noting is the contrast between the anatomical details of the **David** and those of the body of Christ here. As is well known, Michelangelo studied anatomy at length, going so far as to dissect bodies in the leper hospital near the Church of Santo Spirito. Here the muscles of the legs hang flaccid beside the bones. In the abdominal section, tragically elongated, in the representation of the rib cage, in the position of the head, one can see that this is a dead body already past the stage of rigor mortis. Involved in his sorrowful contemplation of the dead Christ, the artist has left the figures of the Virgin and Mary Magdalene in the shade, barely sketched in, almost as if they were out of focus.

St. Matthew

The statue of St. Matthew (after whom the Academy itself is named) was part of a series of the 12 Apostles which Michelangelo was to have sculpted for the Cathedral of Santa Maria del Fiore. But the artist's contract with the Wool Guild was annulled in 1505, and of the series there remains only this imposing figure, which seems almost in the act of freeing itself from the cold, inert material of the marble.

The four Prisoners

Pope Julius II had given instructions to Michelangelo to design and sculpt a monument for his tomb. Apart from the figure of the Pope himself, the monument was to have included the statue of Moses and an unspecified number of other figures representing, for example, the liberal arts, prisoners at the Pope's tomb after his death. After the sudden death of Julius II in 1513, there were long and heated arguments with the Pope's heirs until finally his tomb, reduced in size compared with the original plan, was placed in the Church of St. Peter-in-Chains in Rome. Of the six **Prisoners** which were to have stood on the tomb, four are in the Academy Gallery

here and two in the Louvre in Paris. The four statues remain, like the **St. Matthew,** uncompleted, but their unfinished state constitutes a powerful artistic statement: twisting spasmodically in the marble, the **Prisoners** seem to express the dual nature of man himself, able on the one hand to understand eternal metaphysical values, but always conscious on the other of his earthly limits as a creature imprisoned by Time.

Along the walls of the stand hang superb tapestries made in Flanders and Florence in the 16th and 17th centuries. Their subjects are stories from Genesis, and especially that of Adam and Eve.

CALCIO IN COSTUME
(FOOTBALL IN PERIOD COSTUME)

In the month of June, on the occasion of the festival of St. John the Baptist, the patron saint of Florence, the three matches of traditional football in period costume are played in Piazza Signoria. The teams represent the city quarters of San Giovanni, Santa Croce, Santa Maria Novella and Santo Spirito. Famous matches of this game, like the one played in winter on the frozen Arno, are documented from as early as the 15th century. The game is preceded and followed by historical processions, in which members of ancient and noble Florentine families take part, wearing splendid 16th-century costumes. (The photograph above left is of the marquis, Emilio Pucci). The prize for the winner, just as it was in the 16th century, is a roast calf, to be eaten by the victorious quarter.

PIAZZA SIGNORIA

This austerely beautiful square, dominated by the majestic Palazzo Vecchio, or Palazzo della Signoria, has always been the political centre of Florence and the meeting-place of its people. Here developments in affairs of state were made public, here wars were declared, here foreign dignitaries were ceremoniously received and heroes honoured. In short, for many centuries the most important historical and political events took place in this square, including the hanging of those who took part in the Conspiracy of the Pazzi (1478) and the unjust execution of Girolamo Savonarola and two other Domenican friars (1498). Piazza Signoria, with its unforgettable suggestions of power and greatness, saw the internal struggles for political control in Florence, the gradual affirmation of the city's might, and the spread of its splendid culture throughout the world.

THE FOUNTAIN OF NEPTUNE

Designed and sculpted for the most part by Bartolomeo Ammannati, it was unveiled in 1565 on the occasion of the marriage between Francesco I dei Medici and Giovanna d'Austria. Dominating the fountain in the centre is the huge mass of Neptune, christened by the Florentines " Il Biancone " (Big White Man). The bronze statues around the rim of the fountain, depicting naiads and satyrs, are mostly by Ammannati and Giambologna, followers of Michelangelo.

FLORAL CEREMONY IN HONOUR OF SAVONAROLA

Every year on May 23 the anniversary of the death of Girolamo Savonarola (see page 118) is celebrated in Piazza della Signoria. Leaders of the Domenican order, the Mayor of Florence and representatives of the Italian Government gather at the exact point where the miliant friar and his followers, Domenico Buonvicini and Silvestro Maruffi, were hanged, and flowers are strewn on the commemorative stone.

COPY OF THE "DAVID"

In front of the entrance to the Palazzo Vecchio can be seen a copy of Michelangelo's **David,** placed here in 1910 to substitute the original which had been transferred to the Academy Gallery (see page 40). The statue was conceived of as a symbol of wisdom and an example to the administrators of the State.

HERCULES AND CACUS, a mediocre work by Baccio Bandinelli (1534). The muscles of the figures are so grotesquely exaggerated that the Florentines came to refer to the statue as the " sack of potatoes ".

LOGGIA DELLA SIGNORIA

This building is also called the Loggia dei Lanzi, because in the 16th century it served to lodge the German mercenaries or Landsknechten of Cosimo I, and the Loggia dell'Orcagna, because it was supposed to have been designed by that artist. It is a rare example of late Gothic art which at the same time anticipates the Renaissance. It is the work of architects who also had a hand in the building of the Cathedral, that is, Benci di Cione, Simone di Francesco Talenti and others, and was constructed between 1376 and 1382 for the election and proclamation of the Priors and the Gonfaloniere (Florence's political leaders) and for other state ceremonies. The sculptural masterpieces which stand under the Loggia belong to various epochs, and make the Loggia a magnificent open-air gallery. Particularly worthy of note under the first arch on the left is the **Perseus,** holding the head of the Medusa which he has cut off and from whose blood the winged horse Pegasus will be born: this masterpiece in bronze by Benvenuto Cellini was sculpted between 1545 and 1554 and has stood here ever since. The modelling of the reliefs in bronze on the marble base is so exquisitely done that it suggests the precision of the goldsmith rather than the sculptor's art. Under the right-hand arch is the famous group, **The Rape of the Sabines,** by the Belgian sculptor Giambologna (1583), made from a single block of marble and anticipating with its spiral form the Baroque art of Bernini in Rome.

INTERIOR
OF THE LOGGIA

In this fine view of the Loggia, one can see a series of statues of women from the Roman era standing along the end wall; the statues were acquired by the cardinal Ferdinando dei Medici for the Villa Medici and were later brought to Florence. In the centre of the Loggia is **Menelaus Supporting the Body of** **Patroclus,** a classical sculpture from a Greek original, presented by Pope Pius V to Cosimo I dei Medici and restored by the artist Tacca. Behind it is the **Rape of Polyxena,** by Pio Fedi (1866), whose pupil Bertoldi created the Statue of Liberty in New York. Finally there is another work by Giambologna, **Hercules Battles with the Centaur Nessus** (1599). The Lions at the entrance of the Loggia are (on the right) a work by an unknown Greek sculptor and (on the left) a work by Flaminio Vacca (1600).

PALAZZO VECCHIO

The Palazzo Vecchio, which has become almost the symbol of Florence, is one of the finest medieval public buildings in Italy. It is austere and imposing in appearance, and its tower (305 feet high) soars upwards from the facade, a boldly constructed concept which gives the whole building its peculiarly graceful aspect. Tradition has it that the Palazzo Vecchio was constructed by Arnolfo di Cambio between 1298 and 1314. It is a massive building of rough ashlar-stone, with elegant Gothic mullioned windows on each of the two storeys and a battlemented gallery projecting above. Above the facade is the slim tower, rectangular in plan and with double parapet. On top of the tower are a lily, symbol of Florence, and a lion rampant, which (according to the decree of the city rulers) " just as the cross on the Church means that it is a temple consecrated to God, should symbolise the liberty and the might of the Florentine Republic ". At the base of the tower is a small prison cell called the " Alberghetto ": among its prisoners were the Medici ruler, Cosimo the Elder, and later, in the forty-five days before his sentence to death, Savonarola. The clock, originally made in the 15th century, was restored by Viviani, one of Galileo's pupils.

COURTYARD OF THE PALAZZO VECCHIO

The courtyard, like that of the castle of Poppi, once had a stairway which gave access to the upper floors, and brickwork columns. In 1439 the architect Michelozzo was instructed to replace the columns with others made of stone, and in 1565, for the marriage of Francesco I dei Medici to Giovanna d'Austria, Vasari covered the walls with eighteen views of Austrian cities in honour of the bride, and added the gilded stuccoes to the columns. The porphyry fountain is the work of Battista del Tadda, while the "Winged Boy with a Fish" is a copy of the original by Verrocchio, Leonardo da Vinci's master; the original is now in the Machiavelli Room of the Palazzo Vecchio.

THE HALL OF THE FIVE HUNDRED

After the Medici were driven into exile for the second time in 1494, the friar Girolamo Savonarola gained political control of Florence, and introduced as an important reform the creation of a " Consiglio Generale del Popolo " (General Council of the People), made up of more than a thousand citizens. In order to provide a meeting-place for the council, work was begun on the construction of this so-called Hall of the Five Hundred; Simone del Pollaiolo was put in charge of the project, and Leonardo da Vinci and Michelangelo were later commissioned to paint frescoes on the walls. After Savonarola's violent death and the return of the Medici, the people's council was automatically abolished and work on the Hall interrupted. The Hall as it is today was completed by Giorgio Vasari, who directed the work and had various capable collaborators (1550). The Hall, in the best of 16th-century taste, is 172 feet long and 72 feet wide. The ceiling is divided into 39 panels depicting episodes from the history of Florence and the Grand-duchy of Tuscany: in the centre is the " Triumph of Cosimo I ". Along the upper part of the walls are battle scenes by Vasari; below are tapestries dedicated to St. John the Baptist and made in the Medici workshop, with a series of statues and marble groups between them.

"Victory"
by Michelangelo

One of the lesser known of Michelangelo's works, it was sculpted for the tomb of Julius II. For various reasons, it was never placed on the tomb, and it was inherited by Michelangelo's nephew, Leonardo Buonarroti, who presented it to Cosimo I dei Medici. The youthful figure of Reason which dominates Brute Force is noteworthy for the elegance of the body and the beauty of the face.

Room of Clement VII

The political importance of this room today lies in the fact that it is the private study of the Mayor of Florence. On the left-hand wall can be seen an important view of the city of Florence during the siege of 1529, while the other frescoes depict particular episodes of the siege. The ceiling is divided into nine oval panels, decorated with gilded stuccoes, which depict episodes from the life of Pope Clement VII. The painting above the window shows the engagement of Catherine dei Medici and Henry II of France.

Hercules kills Diomedes

This group, sculpted by Vincenzo de Rossi (1592), is part of a series of statues standing in the Hall of the Five Hundred and illustrating the Labours of Hercules. Hercules was always considered a symbol of strength and virility by the city of Florence and was thus part of the design of the city's official seal.

The Wardrobe Room

This room, known also as the Map Room, was designed to house in the cupboards along its walls part of the treasures of the Medici family and later of their successors, the Lorraines. Dinner services in solid gold, candelabras, cups, and a splendid collection of firearms were kept here until 1830, when they were transferred in part to the National Museum of the Bargello and in part to the Silver Museum in the Palazzo Pitti. The fine maps were drawn by the Domenican friars Ignazio Danti and Stefano Buonsignori (1570). They include 53 maps of outstanding geographical interest and cover four continents.

The Penelope Room

This room was part of the private apartments of Eleonora of Toledo, daughter of the Viceroy of Naples and wife of Cosimo I dei Medici. The ceiling, painted by Stradano, contains stories of Ulysses and his beautiful wife, Penelope. In the room are tapestries, a chest and a splendid sandstone fireplace. The Madonna and Child with St. John is attributed to Botticelli.

Room of the Lilies

So-called because of the golden lilies which adorn the walls. It has a lacunar ceiling, and on the left-hand wall are frescoes by Domenico del Ghirlandaio (1481) which depict Roman heroes, San Zanobi (an early archbishop of Florence), and two lions with the standard of Florence. (See photograph next page.).

Bust of Niccolò Machiavelli

A coloured terra-cotta bust of the author of the famous political tract, " The Prince ", containing Machiavelli's idea of the perfect ruler of an Italian state in the early 16th century.

Detail of the quarters of Leo X

The grand-duke Cosimo among the artists of his time. Around Cosimo (from left) are Bernardo Tasso, with the model of the Loggia del Mercato Nuovo, Nanni Ungaro and Sanmarino. The two with the beards are Bartolomeo Ammannati and Baccio Bandinelli, followed by Vasari, Benvenuto Cellini and Niccolò Pericoli, called " il Tribolo ", with the plan for the fountains of the Villa Medici di Castello. In the oval panel a portrait of Giovanni, Cosimo's son.

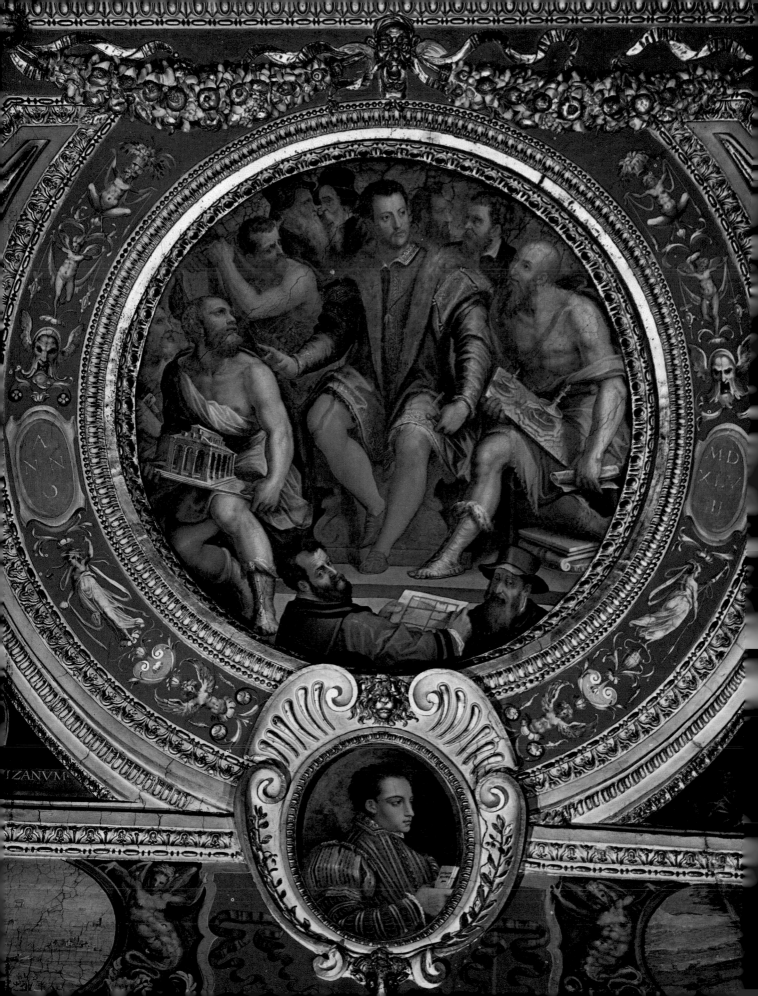

THE UFFIZI GALLERY

The gallery stands next to the Palazzo Vecchio, and is built on the remains of the Romanesque church of San Pietro Scheraggio, some of which can be seen in the vestibule outside the gallery itself. The gallery is designed in the form of a horseshoe, and was originally built so as to bring together under the same roof the administrative and political offices and the law-courts of the Grand-duchy of Tuscany. Its construction was begun in 1560 by Giorgio Vasari, commissioned by Cosimo I dei Medici. The building was completed in 1580, including the long corridor which runs across the top of the Ponte Vecchio, and links the Uffizi Gallery with the Palazzo Pitti.

Later, in a project conceived by Francesco I dei Medici, the covered terrace, the " Tribune " and the adjacent rooms were organised to serve as an art gallery, while the offices and archives were relegated to the lower floor. Later still, Ferdinando I and Cosimo II had new rooms built to accommodate the many works of art which they added to the gallery. Over the last hundred years the gallery has been further enlarged and reorganised along more modern lines. Tapestries and marble works arc displaycd in thc long corridors, while the paintings are hung in chronological order in the adjacent rooms.

FIRST CORRIDOR

Above left can be seen portraits of emperors, kings, queens, cardinals and other illustrious figures. Along the walls are superb tapestries from Flanders and from the Medici workshop in Florence, whose subjects are the months of the year and stories from the life of Catherine dei Medici. There are various Roman busts, among them those of Trajan, Nero and Agrippina, and many sarcophagi. The ceilings are decorated in grotesque style by Butteri, Pieroni and helpers.

Madonna Enthroned, by Cimabue

This large and important work comes from the Church of Santa Trinità in the Vallombrosa, and belongs to the artist's early period, datable at around 1280. The Madonna's clothing belongs clearly to the Byzantine tradition, but the suggestion of perspective and the aristocratic, slightly arrogant expressions of the prophets seem to anticipate a new era and more profound psychological interests.

The Adoration of the Magi, by Gentile da Fabriano

This panel also comes from the Church of Santa Trinità and is dated 1423. In its meticulous representa-

tion of the clothing and fabrics, in its minute, almost fable-like version of reality reminiscent of the miniatures, in the graciousness of the gestures depicted, it reveals the artist's contacts with the northern Italian schools and a tendency towards the International Gothic style.

Madonna Enthroned, by Giotto

Presumably painted around 1310, it comes from the Church of Ognissanti in Florence. As painter, sculptor and architect but above all as a master of the art of fresco, Giotto revolutionised and gave new life to Italian painting, freeing it from the stylised formulas of the Byzantines. Although this altar-piece from Ognissanti obeys the canons of symmetry and proportion dictated by religious tradition, it reveals a continual interest in the individual and expresses a profound humanity.

Madonna and Child with Saints, by Domenico Veneziano

Painted for the Church of Santa Lucia dei Magnoli, this altar-piece dates from about 1445. Although the artist was Venetian in origin, his work has clearly Florentine qualities, such as the incisive design, the geometric perspective of the countryside and the careful study of the light. Here the oblique ray from the sun spreads a diffused light over the figures and objects.

The Coronation, by Beato Angelico

Brought here from the Church of Santa Maria Nuova in Florence, it was painted in 1430. Although still vaguely reminiscent of the elegant illuminated manuscripts and of the last Giottesque painters, the painter clearly had contact with the new generation of sculptors and architects like Brunelleschi and Donatello. The work has a gold background in the 14th-century manner but at the same time a Renaissance maturity. Beato Angelico was a saintly man and a masterly artist. The pure spiritual quality of his inspiration makes him a unique phenomenon in the early Renaissance.

The Battle of San Romano, by Paolo Uccello

Painted for Cosimo the Elder in about 1456, this is the central part of three panels. This comes from the Palazzo Medici, where with the other two panels (one now in the Louvre in Paris and the other in the National Gallery in London), it was hung in the rooms of Lorenzo the Magnificent. It was painted in honour of the Florentine military leader, Niccolò da Tolentino, after his victory over the Sienese. The battle-scene is surprisingly modern in its abstract formalism, in its free use of colours which do not correspond to reality, and in the insistent utilisation of a rigorously geometric perspective which seems to arrest the violence of the subject. " A capricious and imaginative painter ", Vasari was to call Paolo Uccello, who today seems a precursor of modern art.

Portrait of a Gentleman, by Botticelli

The masterpiece of the artist's period under the influence of Pollaiolo. With his precise line, Botticelli reproduces exactly the face and the graceful bearing of the subject. The medallion depicts the Medici ruler Cosimo the Elder.

Portrait of a Woman, by Antonio Pollaiolo

The incisive line and the vivid colours give the work a special sort of vitality. The profile stands out clearly against the blue of the sky, expressing not only the beauty of the subject but almost her awareness of being beautiful.

In the last part of his life, the artist devoted himself above all to sculpture. In his agile figures, such as the Hercules and Antheus in the Bargello, he uses all the means at his disposal to express mobility rather than structure.

Madonna and Child, by Filippo Lippi

Filippo Lippo's reputation as the " merry friar " is at least equal to his fame as a painter. Born in Florence in 1406 and placed in the Carmine monastery while still a child, he seems to have left the monastery in 1431. As a youth he saw first Masolino and then Masaccio at work, and his early works show clearly the influence of the latter. In the Madonna and Child in the Uffizi, the element of design is so greatly emphasised that it seems almost the artist's only means of expression. His colour creates a soft light, and the play of light and shade, plus the transparency of the veils, creates the illusion of movement rather than of substance. In the context of this soft light, the suggestion of modelling in the face of the Madonna seems hardly more than a tremor.

The delicate profile of the Virgin Mary, seated by the window, is outlined clearly against the rocky landscape, while two angels hold up the Christ Child, who reaches toward his praying Mother. The angel in the foreground turns with an odd smile towards the spectator.

The Allegory of Spring and the Birth of Venus, by Botticelli

Botticelli's intellectual formation can partly be explained by the cultural interests in the Humanist circle of the Medici, the artist's great patrons, but it stemmed above all from his acute sensibility and the impressionable nature of his character. Naturally inclined to contemplation and meditation, Botticelli seemed sickly to his father, who registered him as a dependent in his taxation declaration. How-

ever, Lorenzo the Magnificent was extremely fond of the artist, and Botticelli succeeded in giving form to his ideals of beauty, exalting their intellectual value " through cogitation and extreme subtlety ". The Medici turned to him for designs for their tapestries and for both religious and non-religious paintings. Botticelli left a record of the elegant and refined Florence of the 15th century, expressed at times with graceful languor, at times with an almost melodic or rhythmical beauty, and at times — in his later paintings — with surprisingly dramatic violence.

The allegories, the tondi and the mythological scenes in the Uffizi constitute the most important col-

lection of Botticelli's works in the world. In the allegory of **Spring,** painted in 1477 for Lorenzo di Pierfrancesco dei Medici, there are echoes of the verses of Poliziano and of the ideals of the classical world which he had assimilated, echoes of a Florence resounding with festivals and songs, and of the loves of the beautiful Simonetta and the handsome Giuliano. In the **Birth of Venus,** the goddess of Beauty, painted with a precise outline in a complex rhythm of curves, is borne by the winds to land from the Aegean Sea. Subtly melancholy and musical qualities give this poetic painter, with his highly personal range of colour tones, his peculiar fascination.

Adoration of the Shepherds, by Hugo Van Der Goes

This is the Portinari Tryptych, the most important work by this Flemish artist. It was painted in 1486 for the Florentine banker, Tommaso Portinari, who can be seen with members of his family as spectators of the sacred scene, and was destined for the Church of Sant'Egidio in Florence. The work influenced various Florentine artists (among them Ghirlandaio and Filippino Lippi), who were fascinated by its luminous colours and naturalistic details. The joy of the shepherds on seeing the Christ Child is clearly expressed.

Annunciation, by Leonardo da Vinci

The attribution of this work to Leonardo was disputed at length by critics in the past. If indeed it is by his hand, it belongs to his Florentine period when he was in the workshop of Verrocchio along with Botticelli and Perugino. Though only in his twenties, Leonardo had already left behind the rather wooden, curly-haired figures of Verrocchio, creating a new type

of angel with calm, somewhat feminine features. In the Tuscan landscape, dominated by the cypress tree, one can already seen the delicate shading with which Leonardo softened his geometric perspective and created magnificent aerial, almost transparent, effects. At the same time, in the misty distances of the background compared with the rigorously exact representation of the lawn on which the angel kneels and of the angel's wings, one can detect echoes of Leonardo's scientific investigations into man and nature. On the other side of the table, which is reminiscent of Verrocchio, sits the serene and beautiful figure of the Virgin.

The Adoration of the Magi, by Leonardo da Vinci

This is another work from the youthful period of Leonardo. He was given the commission by the friars of San Donato at Scopeto in 1481, and the work was interrupted when he left Florence for Milan. The calm figures of the Virgin and Child, emanating a divine serenity, contrast with the excited confusion of the crowd of spectators, separated from them by a zone of shade.

Angelo Allori, called Bronzino

In the "Tribune" of the Uffizi there are numerous portraits by Bronzino who was the official court painter for Cosimo I. The portraits of the two children of the Medici household (perhaps Cosimo's own children) give an idea of the artist's aesthetic sense and precision.

Angel with Lute, by "il Rosso"

Giovan Battista di Jacopo, called "il Rosso" (the Redhead) because of the colour of his hair, was a Mannerist painter with an original and fecund imagination. In this work he displays a fresh new sense of invention, very different from the classical, decorative tastes of his age.

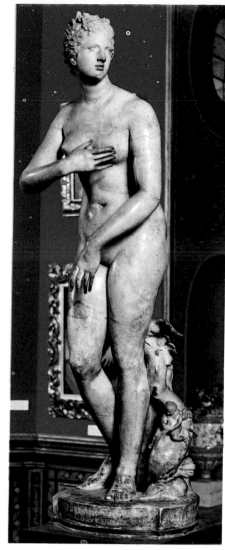

The " Tribune " of the Uffizi

This is a room built on an octagonal plan by Buontalenti (1585-89) with the aim of displaying the gallery's most precious and greatly admired works. The cupola was decorated with mother-of-pearl shell by Poccetti. Among the various marbles groups exhibited here, the most outstanding is the **Medici Venus,** discovered during excavations of Hadrian's Villa at Tivoli, near Rome, and brought to Florence during the reign of Grand-duke Cosimo III. The octagonal drawing table, with its extremely intricate design, is one of the finest examples of the mosaic art in Florence, inlaid with semi-precious stones; designed by Lingozzi and Poccetti (17th cent.), it took 16 years of work.

Detail of the grotesque decorations (16th century)

This sort of decoration, of a joyous, ornamental character, derives from the "Domus Aurea" or so-called grottoes of Nero. In it human figures and animal and vegetable forms are used in extravagant and whimsical combinations.

Flemish tapestry from the 16th century

This is part of a series of tapestries woven in the Belgian city of Brussels in the 16th century, depicting celebrations held by Henry II of France and his wife Catherine dei Medici in Paris.

THE PONTE VECCHIO

From the side window of the gallery, there is a splendid view of the Ponte Vecchio, reflected in the waters of the Arno as the river runs down towards Pisa. The bridge is called Ponte Vecchio (" Old Bridge ") because it is the oldest of all in Florence; indeed there was a bridge here as far back as the time of the Etruscans. There is record of a wooden bridge here in 972; later destroyed and rebuilt in stone, it was destroyed once more by the savage flood in 1333. The present structure is that of Neri di Fioravante, who rebuilt the bridge, once again in stone, in 1345. The picturesque little shops which line it were once occupied by butchers, but in the 16th century by order of Cosimo I they were assigned to the silversmiths and goldsmiths who still sell their wares here. Above the shops on the left-hand side runs the famous corridor built by Vasari to link the Uffizi Gallery on one side of the river with the Palazzo Pitti on the other. On the facades of the buildings on the left bank of the river can still be seen the signs of Florence's disastrous flood in 1966.

The Shepherd Martius (Boy with a thorn)

This is a Roman copy of the fine Greek original in bronze, which can be seen in the Capitoline Museums in Rome.

Madonna of the Goldfinch, by Raphael

This delicate Madonna, reminiscent of Raphael's " La Belle Jardinière " in the Louvre in Paris, was painted by Raphael in 1506 during his Florentine period for the aristocrat Lorenzo Nasi. The painter had already left behind the Umbrian influence of Perugino, and the almost affected, rather somnolent images gain a new poetic beauty from the fine shading technique of Leonardo and the compositive sureness of Fra Bartolomeo. In the pyramidal form of the group and in the delicate rendering of the landscape can be seen that absence of passion which was to remain typical of Raphael's work.

The Venus of Urbino, by Titian

This canvas came into the possession of the Medici through the marriage of Vittoria della Rovere, of Urbino, to Ferdinando II dei Medici. An early work by Titian, it seems to take its inspiration from the Dresden Venus by Giorgione, Titian's first master.

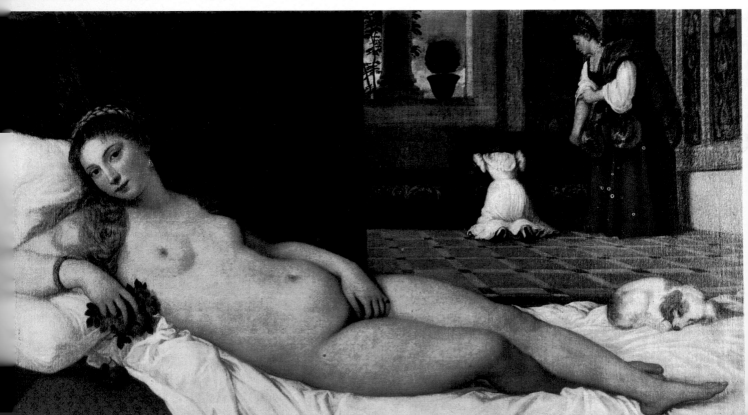

Sacred Family, by Michelangelo

This is the famous " Doni tondo ", painted by Michelangelo for the marriage of Angelo Doni and Maddalena Strozzi. It was painted in 1506, shortly after the completion of the **David.** It was later acquired by the Medici family, and in 1635 was already part of the Uffizi collection. In the versatile genius of Michelangelo, painter, sculptor and architect, the role of sculptor always seems to dominate. Here the modelling technique recalls that of sculpture, almost as if the work had been painted with the scalpel. The nudes in the background, the position of the Virgin, reminiscent of the classical figures of women carrying amphoras, and the marble-like colours similar to stone mosaics all confirm the artist's natural inclination towards sculpture. The sense of movement and energy in the complex composition of the painting give it exceptional strength. The splendid frame is the original one placed around the work.

LOGGIA OF THE NEW MARKET

Cosimo I had the loggia built in 1547 to a design by G. B. del Tasso to accommodate the merchants, money-changers and weavers of wool and silk who displayed their goods here. The carrying of arms in the market area was severely prohibited. Information on the sailing dates of ships from Pisa and Livorno was also to be had in the loggia. Today the stalls of the "Straw Market" are here. The bronze fountain was placed at the end of the loggia by Ferdinando II. The wild boar on it, commonly referred to as the "Porcellino" (little pig), was cast by Pietro Tacca in 1612, inspired by a Hellenistic original which is in the Uffizi. Its base was restored last century.

BASILICA OF SANTA CROCE

This is the largest and most illustrious Franciscan church in Italy. Its construction was begun in the second half of the 13th century on the remains of a chapel which had been built here in 1228 by the Franciscan Friars Minor. The ruins of the chapel have come to light recently during restoration work following the flood in 1966. The design of Santa Croce is attributed by tradition to Arnolfo di Cambio, who was also the architect of Florrence's Cathedral and the Palazzo Vecchio. It has been enriched over the centuries by so many artistic masterpieces that today it is virtually an art gallery. It also contains the remains of many great Italians, so that in a sense it is reminiscent of Westmister Abbey in London. The facade is a more modern work by Niccolò Matas (1857-1863), as is the statue of Dante Alighieri by Enrico Pazzi (1865), recently moved from the centre of the square to a position to one side of the facade.

INTERIOR OF THE BASILICA OF SANTA CROCE

The interior is of impressively grandiose dimensions, designed in the form of an Egyptian cross and divided into three naves with graceful pillars and pointed Gothic arches. The ceiling, as was traditional in Franciscan churches, is of the open-beam design, while the floor is in brickwork. The walls were once entirely covered with frescoes by Giotto and other painters, which would have survived to our own times, except that in the 16th century Giorgio Vasari, as part of a plan to renovate the church, had the

frescoes covered with plaster and placed cumbersome altars of little artistic merit along the walls. From early times, Florentines who had been attracted by the message of humility, poverty and chastity preached by St. Francis were buried here. The church thus became an important burial place, in which many members of noble Florentine families and eminent men of various epochs were laid to rest. An increasing number of funeral monuments, tombstones and commemorative stones came to be placed here over the centuries. Not only were great men in every field buried here, but funeral monuments were erected to those buried elsewhere, as if to attest to their spiritual presence, so that the church has become almost a national shrine.

1) Tomb of Michelangelo (1564), designed by Vasari, with the statues symbolising Painting, Sculpture and Architecture. The bust of Michelangelo was sculpted by Lorenzi.

2) Monument to Dante Alighieri, a work by Stefano Ricci (1830), with the figures of Italy, of Dante himself, and of Poetry weeping for her dearest son.

3) Tomb of Machiavelli, by I. Spinazzi (1859), depicting the famous political theorist and author of " The Prince ".

4) Tomb of Galileo, by Foggini and Ticciati (1642), with figures representing Astronomy and Geometry.

ONORATE L'ALTISSIMO POETA

DANTI · ALIGHERIO
TVSCI
HONORARIVM · TVMVLVM
A · MAIORIBVS · TER · FRVSTRA · DECRETVM
ANNO · M · DCCC · XXIX
FELICITER · EXCITARVNT ·

NEL VII CENTENARIO DELLA
NASCITA
L'ASSOCIAZIONE NAZIONALE
DEI COMUNI ITALIANI
MCCLXV · MCMLXV

NEL VII CENTENA
NASCITA
ASSOCIAZIONE NA
MCCLXV · MCMLXV

TANTO · NOMINI · NVLLVM · PAR · ELOGIVM
NICOLAVS · MACHIAVELLI
OBIT · AN · A · P · V · CIↃIↃXXVII

1

2

1) **The Pulpit** in the central nave was commissioned by Pietro Mellini in 1470 and is the work of Benedetto da Maiano. The splendid bas-reliefs, somewhat reminiscent of those by Ghiberti on the eastern door of the Baptistry, depict episodes from the life of St. Francis of Assisi. Particularly worthy of note are the panels showing the approval of the Franciscan order by Pope Honorius III, the saint receiving the stigmata, and his death. On the floor is a fine work of marble inlay, with stones of different colours, including the escutcheon of the family which donated the work (three blue circles).

2) This splendid sandstone **Annunciation,** with terra-cotta angels above, is by Donatello (1430). The architectural features and the somewhat classical faces of the Virgin and the Angel create an impression of graceful serenity.

3) On the first pillar on the right is the **Madonna and Child** by Antonio Rossellino, sculpted in the second half of the 15th century for the tomb of F. Nori, a follower of the Medici family.

4) The panel depicting **St. Francis,** surrounded by twenty smaller paintings relating episodes from his life, is by unknown artist of the 13th century.

5) Detail of the **Funeral rites of St. Francis,** painted by Giotto in 1317 in the Bardi Chapel. The genius of Giotto in his maturity can be clearly seen here. The tragic scene is depicted with much more calm and authority than in Giotto's earlier fresco in Assisi. It thus succeeds in expressing noble resignation and at the same time the certainty of faith.

3

4

THE SACRISTY

On the right-hand side of the church is the entrance to the sacristy, built at the expense of the Pazzi and Rinuccini families. It expresses perhaps better than the church as a whole the original Franciscan concept of simplicity. The cupboards, the cabinet in the centre and the illuminated manuscripts have been restored recently following the flood in 1966 in which the water reached a height of nearly 15 feet in the square in front of the church. The frescoes on the walls, attributed to the Giottesque painter Niccolò di Piero Gerini, depict the Ascent to Calvary, the Crucifixion and the Ascension; they have been restored several times. On the left is a fine wrought-iron partition which bears the date 1371. On the other side of it is the Rinuccini Chapel, with its outstanding frescoes by Giovanni da Milano (1365). The picture on the right shows the main altar and the apse, with frescoes by followers of Giotto.

The Cathedral of Santa Maria del Fiore, seen from the entrance to the Boboli Gardens; on the left-hand side, the Palazzo Pitti.

Sunset on the Arno, with the towers of the Palazzo Vecchio and Santa Croce and the cupola of the Cathedral reflected in the river.

PALAZZO PITTI

This grandiose structure, built on the hill of Boboli, was the imposing residence of the Grand-dukes of Tuscany, and later of the Kings of Italy when Florence was Italy's capital in 1865. It was originally designed by Filippo Brunelleschi in the first half of the 15th century for Luca Pitti, an extremely rich Florentine merchant, who not only wanted a residence more sumptuous than all the others then standing in Florence, but gave instructions that its windows should be as big as the entrance doorway of the Medici family's residence in Via Larga (what is now the Palazzo Medici-Riccardi in via Cavour). Brunelleschi designed the central section in his typical measured Renaissance style, with simple but imposing forms reminiscent of the Etruscan walls in Fiesole. The walls are in ashlar or rustic-style stone, and on the level of each of the three storeys are the huge archways of the windows. In 1465, when the Pitti family fell into financial ruin, work was interrupted on the building. In 1549 it was acquired by the first Medici Grand-duke, Cosimo I, for his wife, Eleanor of Toledo, and Bartolomeo Ammannati was commissioned to complete the construction; the work, carried out between 1558 and 1570, created a building on a larger plan, which however substantially respected Brunelleschi's original style. In the following century, the facade was once more extended by Giulio Parigi (1620), and later Alfonso Parigi, the son of Giulio, completed it to its present dimensions and appearance. The two side wings were added between 1764 and 1783 on a design by Giuseppe Ruggieri. Previously the residence of the Medici and then of the Lorraine Grand-dukes, Palazzo Pitti was the palace of the Savoy Royal family until 1871. The facade as it is today is 765 feet long and 117 feet high in the centre, and the building occupies an area of nearly 350,000 square feet. The side entrance to the left gives access to the Treasure Museum, the Palatine Gallery and the Royal apartments, the central entranceway to the Gallery of Modern Art on the second floor, the door on the right under the arches to the Museum of Carriages, which can be seen on request. Extending far back behind the Palazzo Pitti are the Boboli Gardens, a splendid example of the Italian-style garden of the 16th century, later imitated throughout Europe.

PIAZZALE DELL'ISOLOTTO
(Square of the Little Island)

Planned by Tribolo and built by Alfonso Parigi
(1618), this section of the garden has the largest
pool of all its fountains. The gates with their four
columns, on which stand statues of ibexes (a symbol
of Cosimo I), give access to the island, which is
planted with citrus trees and has Giambologna's
Fountain of the Ocean in the centre. The basin of
the fountain is made of granite from the island of
Elba and is 73 feet in circumference. In the foreground
can be seen statues of Andromeda chained to the cliff
and behind this Perseus, by Giambologna.

FOUNTAIN OF BACCHUS

Situated near the entrance at the corner of the left-
hand wing of the palace. The little fat dwarf, seated astride a turtle, was sculpted by Valerio Ciolo,
who used Cosimo I's celebrated court jester, Pietro
Barbino, as his model.

PALATINE GALLERY

In contrast with the other art galleries in Florence,
which have been organised in chronological order
along modern scientific lines, the Palatine Gallery
has been left in its original condition as a series of

luxurious and richly decorated rooms. It thus reveals the tastes of its one-time owners and of their epochs. The many important works of art which it contains are displayed in pleasant disorder. In its rooms, adorned with stuccoes, frescoes and tapestries, there are masterpieces by Raphael, Rubens, Murillo, Velasquez, Titian, Veronese and others.

ILIAD ROOM

This takes its name from the frescoes in the vault, painted in 1819 by Luigi Sabatelli and depicting scenes from the Trojan War in Homer's **Iliad.**

Prince Waldemar, son of the King of Denmark, by Sustermans

A native of Antwerp in Flanders and follower of Van Dyck, Sustermans became a portrait painter in the Grand-duke's court in Florence. Remaining faithful to the traditions of Flemish painting, he painted many meticolous portraits, trying always to obtain the most exact likeness possible of his subjects.

Cardinal Tommaso Inghirami, by Raphael

This portrait, painted in Rome in about 1510, shows the eminent man of letters and librarian of Pope Leo X with an absorbed expression, in the act of writing. An exceptional work for its fullness of vision and vibrant colours, without being excessively grandiose or dramatic.

Table inlaid with semi-precious stones

This table too comes from the Florentine workshop where this fine art was developed. It is of Egyptian porphyry, inlaid with red coral, chalcedony, jasper, agate and other stones. The Greek border around the shell design is of lapis-lazuli.

Madonna of the Chair, by Raphael

Previously hung in the " Tribune " in the Uffizi Gallery (it was there as early as 1589), this masterpiece was transferred to the Palatine Gallery at the end of the 17th century. The tondo is perhaps Raphael's most popular work, painted around 1515 when he was working on his frescoes in the Villa Farnesina in Rome. The artist, always intensely aware of the world around him, at times profitted considerably from the experiences of the brilliant group of artists which Papal patronage continually drew to Rome. The monumental splendour of Michelangelo and the warm colour tones from the palette of Sebastiano del Piombo are combined in Raphael's vision to express his concept of beauty, based on the harmony of proportions and the complete absence of passion. The appeal of this work lies in its splendid colours and in the warm, golden flesh and Latin beauty of the figures depicted.

TVBVM OPTICVM VIDES GALILAEI IN...VM ET OPVS, QVO SOLIS MACVLAS,
ET EXTIMOS IVNAE MONTES, ET I...ATELLITES, ET NOVAM QVASI
RE...NIVERSITATE...S DISPEXIT A. MDCIX.

Portrait of Galileo, by Sustermans

The famous astronomer Galileo Galilei was born in Pisa in 1564, and
went on to study medicine, philosophy and mathematics there. When
not yet twenty-three years old he invented the hydrostatic balance, and
a few years later, as a teacher at the University of Pisa, he had the courage
to confute Aristotle. His studies of the force of gravity and the pendulum
also belong to this period. After gaining a teaching post in Padua, he
succeeded in developing and perfecting a magnifying glass, which was
later called the telescope. With this instrument, Galileo was to discover
the mountains and seas of the moon, sun-spots, the four planets of Jupiter
and other stars, discoveries published in his work **Sidereus Nuncius** (1610),
dedicated to the Medici ruler Cosimo II. His celebrated **Dialogue,** proving
that the earth is round and that it rotates around the sun, according to
the theories of Copernicus, dates from 1632. This book was to be classi-
fied by the Sacred College in Rome as " more execrable and pernicious
for the Holy Church than the writings of Calvin and Luther ". Galileo
was forced to recant and was sentenced to prison, a sentence later com-
muted to liberty under surveillance, and passed his last years at Alcetri,
near Florence. He died there, after going blind, on 8 January 1642. Galileo's famous telescope, together with others of his inventions, are kept
in the Science Museum in Florence.

Veiled woman, by Raphael

This magnificent portrait of a young
woman came to the Palatine Gallery
in 1844 from the Villa del Poggio
Imperiale in Florence. It belongs to
the same period as the **Madonna of
the Chair** (about 1515), and may
indeed be of the same model,
perhaps the famous Fornarina, the
Roman woman Raphael loved. The
serene, idealised beauty and the
blooming health of the young
woman are emphasised against the
splendid grey silk dress, trimmed
with gold. The mysterious smile
and the position of the hands recall
once again Leonardo's **Mona Lisa.**

The Four Philosophers and The Consequences of War, by P. P. Rubens

Rubens was born in Siegen during the period in which the art of Flanders looked towards Italian art for new inspiration, learning from Italy an admiration for the nude and a love of allegorical paintings. A pupil of the " Romanist " painter Voenius, Rubens came to Italy in 1600, visiting Venice, Mantua, Rome and Florence and making a long and profound study of the works of Titian, Mantegna and Caravaggio. The panel, **The Four Philosophers,** painted in about 1615, contains the self-portrait of the artist above left, with his brother Philip, Justus Lipsius and Jan van der Wouwere, with the bust of Seneca. In the glowing flesh tones and the deliberate effects of colour, Rubens displays his virtuosity, making light of technical difficulties. The other canvas, depicting **The Consequences of War,** was sent by Rubens himself to his compatriot Sustermans in Florence. On the left can be seen Europe in mourning, while Mars, despite the vain attempts of Venus to withhold him, tramples and destroys culture, harmony and architecture. The work is full of the movement and violent contrasts which made Rubens one of the greatest Baroque masters.

Madonna
of the Rosary,
by Murillo

This subject, rather Italian in taste,
was painted many times, The canvas
suggests the devout nature of this
artist's work.
There are almost 500 known works
by his hand in the galleries of various cities, including Madrid, Sevil-
le, Paris, Leningrad and Florence.

Portrait of an English Gentleman and Mary Magdalene, by Titian

These two works almost certainly come from the inheritance of Vittoria della Rovere, of Urbino, wife of Ferdinando II dei Medici. The " English gentleman ", said by some to be the Duke of Norfolk, by others to be Ippolito Rimanaldi of Ferrara, is different from the early portraits by Titian which were permeated by the somewhat romantic

vision of his master Giorgione. Here the artist's interest is essentially psychological, and he concentrates his attention on the face and the hands of the subject, creating an extremely concrete likeness. The figure stands out against the even colour of the background in a cool, almost transparent atmosphere. The **Mary Magdalene** has all the most important features of Titian's style, such as the gilded richness of his colour and the monumental composition. The figure is surrounded by the golden cloud of her hair, under the lapis-lazuli of the sky. On the left, in the hollow of the vase, can be clearly seen the word, " Titianus ", the artist's signature.

Peasants Returning from the Fields, by P. P. Rubens

The artist's interest seems to be totally absorbed by various features of the landscape, rather than by the human figures. The luminous clouds, whose light is reflected by the fields, create an outstandingly successful effect of spatial perspective.

Charles I of England and Henrietta of France, by Van Dyck

An extremely precocious painter, Van Dyck was a disciple of Rubens. He succeeded in depicting the formal beauty of the brilliant high-society life from which he took his models, without going on to a more profound psychological analysis. Elegant and refined, his work is sometimes dominated by his technical virtuosity.

Table of the Muses

A unique example of the Florentine mosaic art. It was completed towards 1851 after 14 years' work. In the centre can be seen Apollo and around him the symbols of the Muses. The base, depicting the four seasons, is by Giovanni Dupré.

Madonna and Child, by Filippo Lippi

The photograph reproduces the central part of this tondo in the Palatine Gallery. Painted in about 1452 for Leonardo Bartolini, it depicts the birth of Our Lady in the background; the Virgin in the foreground seems absorbed, almost as if she had a presentiment of her Son's destiny.

DINING ROOM

This room stands at the beginning of the series of Royal apartments occupied by Victor Emmanuel II and his queen, Margherita, during the period when Florence was capital of Italy (1865-1871). Portraits of the Medici by Sustermans alternate with niches containing statues; on the walls are vases of Japanese and Sèvres porcelain. On the backs of the chairs can be seen the escutcheon of the Royal house of Savoy.

Judith, by Cristoforo Allori

Allori represents the Biblical episode of Judith with the head of the giant Holofernes, painting such a rich variety of fabrics — velvets, brocades and silks — with such a lively range of colour tones that the surprisingly vivid colours considerably reduce the macabre effect of the scene.

THRONE ROOM

This too is part of the Royal apartments. The decoration and the furniture are in the Empire style. The tapestries by Audran depict stories of the Biblical figures, Queen Esther and King Ahasuerus. Against the wall is the Royal throne. Near the fireplace are ancient Chinese and Japanese vases of considerable value.

Above the doors are the portraits of Henry IV and Mary of France. The frescoes on the ceiling, depicting Jupiter between Juno and Minerva, and paintings on the walls are by P. Sarti and G. Castagnoli.

ROOM OF THE SILVER MUSEUM

On the ground floor, this section of the Palazzo Pitti was reorganised in 1919 to accommodate the Silver Museum. It consists of several rooms with impressive frescoes representing false architectural features and stories of the Medici family, painted by Giovanni da San Giovanni, Furini, Cecco Bravo and others in 1635, on the occasion of the marriage between Ferdinando II dei Medici and Vittoria della Rovere. In the museum there is a rich collection of various objects made of gold, silver, ivory, amber and semi-precious stones. There are numerous cameos, clocks and curious articles of jewellery made by the Florentine goldsmiths. Among the objects made from semi-precious stones the most noteworthy are 16 valuable vases with ornaments and silver bases, which belonged to Lorenzo the Magnificent. The lapis-lazuli vase made by Bernardo Buontalenti for Francesco I dei Medici is of exquisite workmanship, extraordinarily large dimensions and incalculable value. Also worth seeing is the collection of porcellain, lacquered ware, rings, seals and other objects.

NATIONAL MUSEUM OF THE BARGELLO

This is one of Florence's most important medieval buildings. Begun in 1256, some years before the Palazzo Vecchio, it was originally the seat of the " Capitano del Popolo " (magistrate acting in the people's interests) and later of the " Podestà " (head of government). In the 16th century it became the head quarters of the police chief, known as the " Bargello ", from which it derives its name. Today it contains the National Museum, which includes the city's most important collection of Renaissance sculpture, besides ceramics, coins, arms and ivory works.

Among the most famous works of sculpture are:

1) The Madonna and Child with St. John, an exquisite marble tondo by Michelangelo (1504); **2) Bust of Brutus,** seeming to reflect the determination expressed in the political theories of Machiavelli, by the same artist; **3) St. George,** by Donatello, which once stood in the Church of Orsanmichele as the patron saint of the armourers; **4) The Young David,** by Verrocchio, a slim and elegant figure; **5) David,** by Donatello, a work with classical reminiscences and a pensive air; **6) The Drunken Bacchus,** unsure on his feet, an early work by Michelangelo.

Madonna and Child and Madonna of the Apple, by Luca della Robbia

Among the various works by Luca Della Robbia displayed in the Salone del Consiglio Generale, these two versions of the Madonna and Child, with their splendid frames in Luca's unmistakeable style, are the most noteworthy. In the flowing garments, vaguely reminiscent of Ghiberti and in keeping with Luca's serene vision, and in their secure sense of form, these are very much Renaissance works. Such serene expression and delicate modelling can be found only in Luca Della Robbia, perhaps the most classical of all the 15th-century artists.

Sacrifice of Abraham, by Ghiberti and Brunelleschi

These two panels depicting the sacrifice of Abraham have great artistic and historical importance, in that they are the famous trial pieces presented by Lorenzo Ghiberti and Filippo Brunelleschi in the competition for the right to construct the door of the Baptistry in 1401. The lyrical elegance of Ghiberti's version undoubtedly expresses more coherently than that of Brunelleschi the famous Biblical episode.

PALAZZO STROZZI

This imposing building was begun in 1489 by Benedetto da Maiano and completed by Il Cronaca (in the courtyard and cornice) for the rich banker Filippo Strozzi, who, " being more eager for glory than for money, wanted to have a residence constructed which would bring honour to himself and to his family, within Italy and abroad ". Today it is used for important cultural events and art exhibitions, among them the International Exhibition of Antiques.

COLUMN OF JUSTICE

Placed here in Piazza Santa Trinita by Cosimo I to commemorate the victory of his troops over Filippo Strozzi and the Florentine exiles at Montemurlo. In the background at left is the Palazzo Ferroni, dating from the 13th century, at the end of Via Tornabuoni, the most elegant and sophisticated of Florence's streets.

CHURCH OF OGNISSANTI

The church dates back to 1251, and was constructed together with the monastery in which lived the friars called the " Frati Umiliati ", from nearby Prato. The present facade is by Nigetti (1637), and on it is a fine Della Robbia bas-relief. Inside the church are masterpieces by Botticelli, Ghirlandaio and others. It is also the burial place of members of the family of Amerigo Vespucci, the famous Florentine navigator.

CHURCH OF SAN MARCO

In this large square, planted with trees, there was once the ancient Chapel dedicated to St. Mark the Evangelist. When it passed into the hands of the Domenicans, it was enlarged and the monastery was constructed by Michelozzo in 1437 at the expense of the Medici ruler Cosimo the Elder. The present facade is by G. Pronti (1780), while the wooden door was here in the epoch of Savonarola, at the end of the 15th century.

CHURCH OF SANTO SPIRITO

The church was designed and begun in 1436 by the great architect Filippo Brunelleschi. The measured harmony of the interior is in his typical Renaissance style, and the church contains masterpieces by various famous artists, among them Donatello, Lippi, Ghirlandaio and Lorenzo di Credi.

CHURCH OF THE CARMINE

Built at the end of the 13th century, in 1771 it was destroyed by fire except for the Corsini and Brancacci Chapels, being rebuilt by Giuseppe Ruggieri. In the Brancacci Chapel is the famous series of frescoes begun by Masolino in 1424-1425, continued by Masaccio in 1426-1427, and finally completed by Filippo Lippi in 1481-1485. In the **Payment of the Tribute by Christ,** one of the most highly admired frescoes of all time, Masaccio asserts the authority of his genius. The immobile figures of the Apostles stand around the Redeemer, and the large, silent group draws attention to the central part, where Christ's gesture is immediately imitated by St. Peter with sure faith in his Master. The statue-like relief of the figures and the grave dignity of their actions reveal a belief in the nature and importance of man, a belief already visible in Giotto a hundred years previously and reaffirmed by Michelangelo a hundred years later. Masaccio's imagination brings a new vigour to the art of painting. Lippi, Botticelli, Leonardo, Michelangelo and many others up until the present day have gone to the Brancacci Chapel to stand in mute admiration before his work.

SANTA MARIA NOVELLA

The church is built on the site where, up until the 10th century, the Chapel of Santa Maria delle Vigne stood; it came into the hands of the Domenican order in 1221. Two members of the order, Fra Sisto and Fra Ristoro, began work on the church in 1278, though it was consecrated only in 1420 by Pope Martin V. It is for the most part in the Tuscan Gothic style, and shows how the soaring lines of the Gothic style brought from northern Europe were modified in Italy to conform to the more solid lines of the Romanesque style, so important in Tuscany. **The facade,** however, with its limpid lines in green and white marble, is a product of the Renaissance and of the unmistakeable genius of Leon Battista Alberti. It is without doubt, along with the Palazzo Rucellai, the masterpiece of this architect and man of letters, who sought in its design to harmonise the pointed arches of the Gothic style with the classical Renaissance spirit. The interior, in the form of a Greek cross, is 322 feet long. The arches are built so as to create a perspective with its vanishing point in the apse. The distance between the first two pillars is nearly 50 feet, while towards the chorus they are about 37 feet apart. In the church are works by Masaccio, Ghirlandaio, Lippi, and other important artists.

MUSEUM
OF
SAN MARCO

The museum is in the former monastery of the Domenicans, constructed by Michelozzo in 1436 on a commission from the Medici ruler Cosimo the Elder. As in the courtyard of the Palazzo Medici-Riccardi and the cloister of Sant'Antonino, Michelozzo here adheres firmly to the Renaissance forms of Brunelleschi, even though his classicism has none of the other's passion for archeological research in it. The smooth, flowing lines of the cloister's arches create effects of light and shade which alternate in the

series of vaults. Naturally the religious function and the deliberately spiritual effect of the structure, suggested by the order's Vicar General and perhaps by Beato Angelico himself, qualify these chiaroscuro and plastic impressions. In the library on the first floor, the perspective skilfully created by the columns suggests a more precise and intellectual concept. The history of San Marco is inseparably linked to the figures of the painters, Beato Angelico and Fra Bartolommeo, and the friar Girolamo Savonarola.

The celebrated Angelic Musicians, graceful figures painted with the exquisite precision of a miniature, adorn the frame of the **Madonna dei Linaioli** (Madonna of the Flax-workers), done by Beato Angelico in 1433 and to be seen in the Museum of San Marco.

Annunciation, by Beato Angelico

Beato Angelico's exquisite, almost calligraphic style is simplified, partly for technical reasons, in his frescoes. His precise details are reduced to a minimum, and clear pink and grey tones predominate. Framed by the architecture of Michelozzo, the heralding angel and the Virgin are painted with great simplicity and clarity and a religious inspiration without precedent in the history of art.

Girolamo Savonarola (1452-1498)

Fra Girolamo, born in Ferrara, was for some time prior of the Convent of San Marco. Inspired by an aversion for worldly things and the highest religious ideals, with his example and his obscurely threatening and prophetic sermons he condemned first the corrupt way of life of Florence and then the Church hierarchy in Rome. Ignoring numerous reprimands and contemptuous of danger, he was condemn-

ed to death: together with his fellow friars, Domenico da Pescia and Silvestro Maruffi, he was hanged and burnt in Piazza Signoria on 23 May 1498. The responsibility for his unjust sentence has been attributed by some historians to the Florentines, and by others to Rome. But the final cause of his fall was his deluded belief that he could halt the march of time, and his uncompromising effort to impose on the Italians of the 16th century a conception of life by then outdated. The panel, painted by an unknown artist of the epoch, shows Savona-

rola's execution in Piazza Signoria. The portrait of Savonarola was painted by Fra Bartolommeo.

The last three cells on the left of the first floor of the monastery were part of the private apartments of the Prior of San Marco, and here Savonarola lived when he held this position. First there is the large cell containing the painting by an unknown artist, depicting the execution of the friar, and the monument erected by the city of Florence, a work by Dupré (1878). Next to it is the cell in which the famous Domenican prayed and meditated. Here can be seen the celebrated portrait painted by Fra Bartolomeo, several Bibles in manuscript with annotations, and some texts of political and religious sermons in Savonarola's own hand. There are also the chair and other objects which belonged to the friar, including his cilice (the sackcloth garment for penitence), cowl and banner with the crucifix, which he carried when he delivered his sermons.

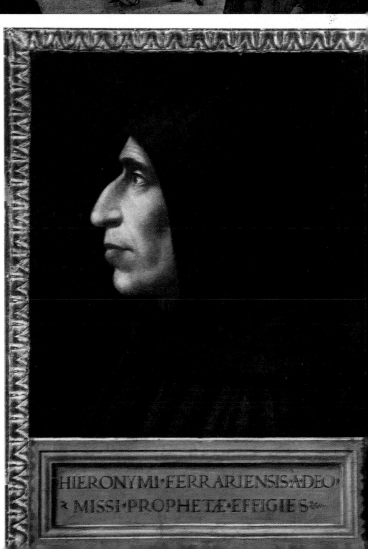

Deposition from the Cross, by Beato Angelico

This panel is considered the artist's masterpiece. It was originally begun by Lorenzo Monaco, commissioned to paint it for the Church of Santa Trinita by Palla Strozzi, and at his death Beato Angelico completed the work. In it, the painter has complete command of his means of expression, and his style reaches the peak of perfection. The naturalistic spirit of the 15th century predominates in this dramatic work, not only in the gestures and expressions of the human figures but above all in the extremely detailed rendering of the landscape, which takes the place of the flat golden backgrounds seen in earlier paintings. Under the vibrant, azure-coloured sky, the architectural forms and the hilly countryside are Tuscan in ispiration. The body of Christ, rendered with great pathos, dominates the clearly articulated central group of figures. The men and women painted here have a sensitive humanity which is different from that of the smaller figures, rapt and estatic, in Beato Angelico's previous works.

THE SYNAGOGUE

This outstanding temple was begun in 1874 to a design by the architects Treves, Falcini and Micheli, and was inaugurated on 24 October 1882 after eight years of intensive work. The construction of such a monumental temple was made possible by a generous legacy left in his will by David Levi, who held the post of president of the council of the Israelite University in Florence from 1860 to 1870. The building is in pure Moorish style; inside there are frescoes throughout and rich Venetian mosaics in the Ehal. Because the great majority of the Florentine Jewish community is of Oriental origin, the official rite is Sephardic Orthodox, while the minority belonging to the Ashkenazi sect worships in a classroom in the school next to the temple. The synagogue was badly damaged during the war and even more so in the flood in 1966, but restoration work has been going on for some time, partly thanks to the help of the enormous quantity of visitors from all parts of the world who come every day to see it.

CHURCH OF SAN MINIATO

It stands on the hill called "Monte alle Croci" (Hill of the Crosses), and from the large square in front of the church there is a magnificent panoramic view of the city and the surrounding hills. The church is in the Florentine Romanesque style with its typical facade of white and dark green marbles, similar to the Baptistry; it was begun in the 11th century. The facade has five archways in the lower part, and above them is a fine window. Above this again there is a large mosaic dating from the 12th century, depicting Christ in the act of blessing between Our Lady and St. Miniato, the saint after whom the church is named. Above the gable, decorated with signs of the zodiac, is the statue of the eagle of the Guild of Calimala, which was responsible for the church for five centuries. The interior, which has three naves and is divided into three distinct areas, is of exceptional interest. The magnificent inlaid floor, dated 1207, which leads to the crypt, seems almost a stone carpet. Worth noting are the Chapel of the Crucifix, by Michelozzo (1448), the frescoes in the sacristy by Spinello Aretino (end of the 14th century), the mosaics in the apse, and the Chapel of the Cardinal of Portugal, with works by Pollaiolo, Della Robbia, Rossellino and others.

PIAZZALE MICHELANGELO

The avenue called Viale dei Colli and the square known as Piazzale Michelangelo were planned by the architect Giuseppe Poggi in 1865 when Florence was the capital of Italy. The splendid avenue, lined with trees, begins at the bridge called Ponte San Niccolò, leads up the Hill of San Miniato to the square, then along the top of the hill past the Torre del Gallo and Arcetri, skirting the Boboli Gardens to lead back down the hill to the city gate called Porta Romana. In the centre of Piazzale Michelangelo is a copy in bronze of the artist's **David,** and of his symbolic statues of Day, Night, Dawn and Dusk.

The monument was presented to the city of Florence by the Italian Government on the occasion of the fourth centenary of the birth of Michelangelo. The square stands 338 feet above sea level, and commands a magnificent view of the city below.

126

FIESOLE

This small Etruscan city, so old that its origins are lost in time, stands between two hills to the north of the Florence. Its magnificent position, from which the entire valley of the Arno can be seen, it works of art and excavations revealing Etruscan and Roman ruins make it an obligatory stopping place for many visitors.

The Roman theatre, discovered in 1809 during excavations of the ancient part of Fiesole, goes back to the time of Silla (1st century B.C.), and was built in the manner of the Greek theatres. From the theatre there is a fine panorama.

INDEX